Contents

Trees, though they are cut and lopped, grow up quickly again.

—Pericles, c. 495-429 BC

What is Pruning?

Pruning involves the selective removal of specific parts of a plant for the benefit of the whole plant. Most commonly, shoots and branches are pruned, but pruning may also be practiced on roots, flower buds, seed heads, or fruits.

There are many reasons to prune trees and shrubs. Pruning can dwarf a plant or make it grow taller; it can open up the canopy of a tree or make it more dense. One unifying principle, however, is that the pruning of ornamentals should modify plant growth in accordance with the natural growth character of the plant. Pruning should be viewed as a regular part of a maintenance schedule, rather than as a remedial correction of long-neglected problems.

For each pruning practice, there are techniques that minimize wounding of the plant and help speed the plant's closure of the wound. A thorough knowledge of pruning is based on an understanding of these techniques, which are described in detail later in this publication.

Why Prune?

Woody ornamental plants may be pruned for a variety of reasons:

- **Maintain plant health and appearance.** Dead, diseased, or injured plant parts should be removed. A dense canopy may be thinned to increase the penetration of air and sunlight. Spindly, crowded stems, as well as suckers and water sprouts, also should be removed. Remove crossing branches to eliminate rubbing off of bark. In planting trees with root systems that have been greatly reduced, the crown may be thinned to re-establish a balance between the top and the roots.

- **Train young plants to enhance their natural form.** Scaffold branches are the primary limbs that form the structure of the canopy. In early training, scaffold limbs can be selected on the basis of their arrangement, angle of attachment, and diameter to enhance tree form and produce mechanically strong plants.

Early training should take advantage of the plant's growth habit, accentuating its natural tendencies, seldom modifying them (Figs. 1, 2).

Figure 1. Tree species with strongly upright, conical growth habit (excurrent); e.g., Liriodendron

Figure 2. Tree species with open, spreading growth habit (decurrent); e.g., Juglans nigra

◆ **Control size.** It is often necessary to keep the size of plants in check by pruning. Benefits may include the reduction of shading by the plant, elimination of interference with utility lines, increased visibility of road signs and traffic, simplified pest control, improved access to flowers or fruit, or simply maintenance of the plant in scale with the surroundings. It is important to realize that while pruning may result in the overall dwarfing of the plant, individual shoots are actually invigorated when some neighboring shoots are removed. When foliage and buds that would develop into leaves are pruned, nutrients and water from the root system are redirected to the remaining growth. The degree to which remaining shoots are invigorated depends on the present vigor of the plant as well as the season in which the pruning is done.

◆ **Influence flowering and fruiting.** Pruning that results in the removal of flower buds will enhance vegetative growth. Thus, flower buds can be completely removed from young plants to allow them to achieve a larger size before the first year of blooming. Conversely, pruning can also be used to stimulate flowering, as on *Buddleia*, *Caryopteris*, *Perovskia*, lilac, and wisteria. These techniques are detailed later in the text.

As a plant matures, it produces more inflorescences and fruit, but they are often smaller. In such cases, pruning can reduce the amount of wood and thus divert energy into larger, though fewer, flowers and fruit.

◆ **Prevent injury to people and/or property.** As a tree grows, the position of a limb on a trunk remains essentially unchanged. Therefore, if the tree is set in a lawn and you intend to mow under it, make sure the lowest limb is above the head of the person who will be mowing. Limbs that overhang structures or parking areas or entangle power lines present real dangers and should be removed. Also, remove any branches that are partially broken and threaten to fall out of the tree. **Any off-the-ground pruning work should be attempted only by professional arborists.**

◆ **Open a vista.** Sometimes we use trees or shrubs to hide an objectionable view in the landscape. In other cases, an attractive scene is hidden from view by overgrown plants. When that happens, the plants can be pruned by one of several methods to restore the vista.

◆ **Rejuvenate old shrubs.** As shrubs mature, they often become leggy and sparse, or twiggy and dense, or develop a profusion of water sprouts from the roots. Any of these conditions can cause a decrease in flower production. To restore such shrubs to their former vigor and size, rejuvenation should be implemented. A hard pruning will also lead to the best color development in shrubs known for their colorful bark, such as yellow twig or red osier dogwood.

◆ **Develop unnatural forms.** It is possible to create many unusual plant forms such as bonsai, topiary, espalier, and pollarding through pruning. Before attempting any of these, however, it is helpful to understand the natural growth habit of the plant and its response to pruning.

◆ **Accentuate natural features.** The bark and branching habit of certain trees and shrubs (e.g., *Stewartia*, *Cornus mas*, *Cornus kousa*) will be more apparent after removal of selected branches or stems.

Timing of Pruning

The time of year in which pruning is done depends upon the type of plant, the desired outcome of the pruning operation, and the severity of the pruning. Remedial pruning to remove broken, dead, or diseased branches can be done at any time of year with little negative effect on the plant.

Another consideration in time of pruning is the rate at which healing takes place. Woody plants do not "heal" in the same way that animals do. Externally, they produce rolls of callus over the wound; internally, they compartmentalize or wall off the damaged tissue from the healthy wood (Fig. 3). These responses to wounding take place most rapidly just prior to the onset of growth in spring (March–April) or just after maximum leaf expansion in mid-June.

Plants are stimulated to produce large quantities of unwanted

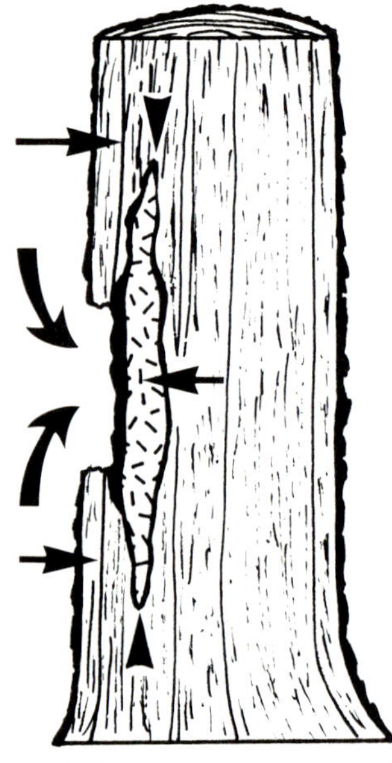

Figure 3. Trees respond to wounding by forming protective boundaries (arrows) that separate infected wood from healthy wood (courtesy of Alex L. Shigo, "New Tree Health").

suckers to a much greater degree by winter or early spring pruning than by late spring or summer pruning. Thus, if suppression of growth is desired, or if the plant naturally suckers heavily, as do lilac and crab apple, summer would be a desirable time to prune.

The susceptibility of plant parts to cold temperature injury may be increased by pruning in late summer. If the pruning is severe enough, it can stimulate late-season growth spurts. Such new growth will be killed back when the weather turns very cold. Also, tissue surrounding winter pruning cuts is more vulnerable to desiccation. This is especially true for certain conifers.

To maximize flowering, first learn the flowering habit of the plant. Trees and shrubs that flower on the current season's wood, such as hydrangea and rose of Sharon, can be pruned before the onset of spring growth. Plants that bloom on the previous season's wood, including ornamental fruit trees and most spring flowering shrubs, should be pruned after the blooming cycle to maximize flowering.

To better understand when specific pruning operations should be done, refer to the Seasonal Pruning Calendar, page 24.

Frequency of Pruning

It is difficult to generalize about how often woody plants should be pruned. Certainly, young, vigorous plants will need more regular prunings than will mature, slow-growing trees or shrubs. Plants that require substantial size control need more frequent pruning than plants being allowed to grow to their natural dimensions.

It may be desirable to perform selective maintenance prunings on flowering or evergreen shrubs on an annual basis. Shade and evergreen trees, once trained, may not need pruning more than once every three or more years, except to remove dead or broken branches. Plants should be pruned only when there is an obvious need, and when you understand what you want to achieve.

Pruning Equipment

You do not need an extensive arsenal of tools to be an expert pruner. One pair of hand pruners, a pair of lopping shears, and a single pruning saw will see you through most pruning operations. Additional tools beyond these three may increase the ease with which pruning jobs can be completed.

Hand pruners (pruning shears, secateurs) can be used to clip off any stems up to 3/4 inch in diameter. There are two main types: a scissors style having sharpened blades that overlap in making the cut, and anvil style that have a sharpened top blade that cuts against a flat plate of softer metal. Scissor types are preferred because they do not crush the bark, and they cut closer to the stem. Anvil pruners may be lighter and less expensive, but they do not provide as clean a cut.

Lopping shears have long handles to provide the leverage needed to cut through branches up to 1 3/4 inches in diameter. Lopping shears are very useful when rejuvenating overgrown shrubs. Ratchet type or geared loppers exert more leverage for cutting thicker limbs, but are considerably more expensive.

A narrow, curved pruning saw can be used on branches up to 2 1/2 inches in diameter where the canopy development is too dense for using a wider saw. There are some new saws from Scandinavia and Japan with tooth designs that can cut very fast and clean. These curved pruning saws allow you to get into seemingly impossible spots and still make professional, clean cuts. They may be expensive and cannot be resharpened, but they will save time and effort.

Pole saws and pole pruners are used to remove overhead branches. Curved pole saws have a stationary blade for removing larger limbs. Pole pruners consist of a stationary hook and hinged blade operated by a rope and chain and mounted on a long wooden or fiberglass pole or series of poles. Pole pruners are useful for branches up to 2 inches in diameter.

Branches 3 inches or greater in diameter can be cut only with coarse-toothed saws or chain saws. Chain saws are available in various sizes and models, powered by gasoline or electricity. In general, the longer the blade and heavier the engine of the chain saw, the larger diameter branch the saw can cut.

On the market today are many models of homeowner chain saws. Any chain saw is dangerous, regardless of its weight. Therefore, all chain saws should be used with caution. Never use the saw above shoulder height. Training is recommended before using or servicing a chain saw.

No matter which pruner, lopper, or saw one uses, the fundamentals for making the pruning cut remain the same: always cut just to the outside of the branch bark ridge, and use a three-cut method (described later) when removing larger branches.

A tool in a category by itself is the electric or manual hedge clipper. Unlike the previously described tools used to make individual pruning cuts, hedge clippers shear off growth in a straight line, without regard to the locations of nodes or bark ridges. Because of this, the use of hedge clippers should be restricted to the annual trimming of thin-stemmed hedges. Even when used in this manner, yearly clippings cause hedge plants to develop a thick profusion of twigs around their perimeter, excluding light and leaf development from the interior. When the time and labor savings offered by hedge clippers is not a consideration, hedge plants will be healthier and more natural looking when trimmed with hand pruners.

Anyone who manages a number of woody plants soon learns that pruning is a lifelong endeavor. In light of this, there is simply no reason to purchase cheap tools that won't be around for the long term. Good tools make pruning more pleasurable and may last as long as you do.

When you purchase quality tools, give them appropriate care. Dry the blades after each use and prevent rust by rubbing them with a few drops of all-purpose oil. Never leave pruning tools outdoors, exposed to the elements. Before starting a vigorous pruning period, sharpen the blades of your pruning tools on a whetstone. Alternately, have the teeth on your chain or hand saw professionally sharpened.

Pruning Deciduous Trees

Certain tasks in tree pruning, such as thinning out, removing a large limb from a mature specimen, or working near utility lines, are best left to a professional arborist. The arborist will have both the technical training and proper equipment to perform the job correctly and *safely*. Practices that can be performed from the ground, such as early training and removal of lower limbs, are appropriate for either the home owner or a professional.

Before studying the particulars of tree pruning, it is helpful to understand the basic anatomy of a tree. The framework of the above-ground portion of a tree consists of the trunk, from which emerge the main scaffold branches and laterals (Fig. 4). At the top of the trunk there is usually a single leader. Suckers emerge at or near the base of the trunk, while water sprouts are shoots that originate along the branches, normally at the sites of pruning cuts.

A branch has little structural or conductive connection to the trunk above it; branch tissue turns abruptly at its base and extends down the trunk. Each year, both the branch and trunk lay down new xylem tissue. This creates a swollen area at the branch base, referred to as the branch collar or shoulder.

The branch bark ridge is the point where the branch collar ends and the branch tissue begins. It is a strong protective zone for preventing decay from entering the trunk. When making pruning cuts in trees or shrubs, always make them in a line just beyond the branch bark ridge (Fig. 5, line A-B). If the branch collar is not obvious, start the cut at the outer edge of the branch bark ridge and cut down and away, at an angle to the ridge.

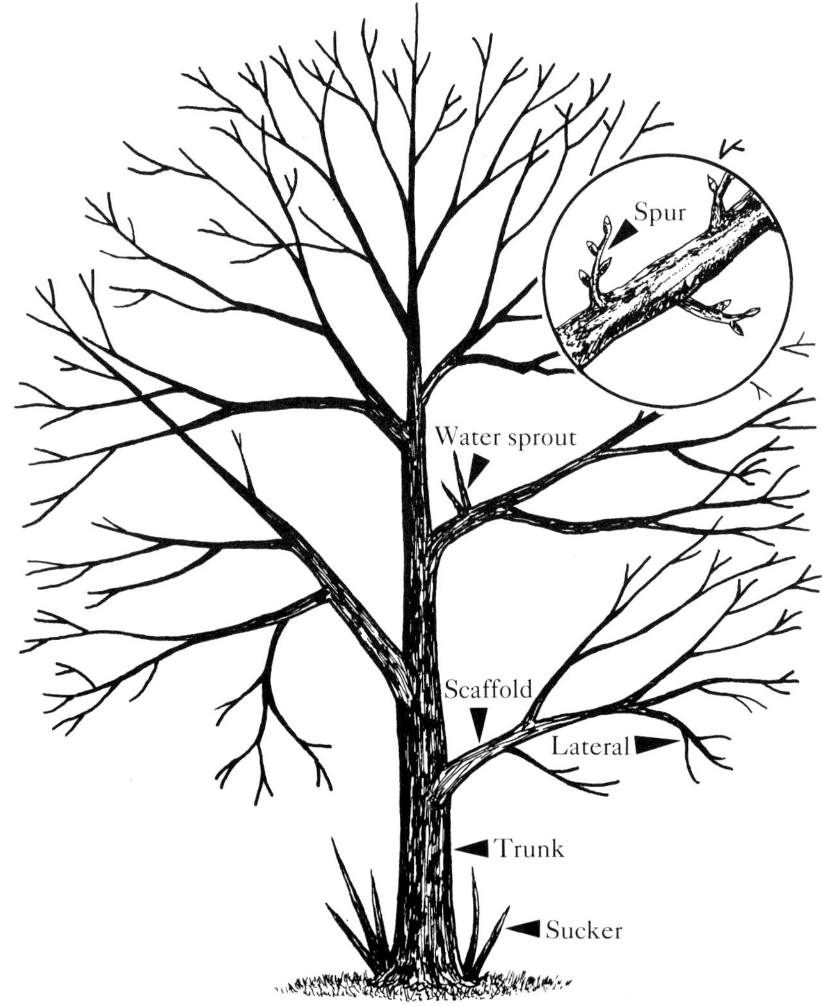

Figure 4. Typical above-ground tree framework.

Before the 1970s, it was standard practice to coat all pruning wounds with an asphalt-based tree paint. Experimental work showed that wound dressings do not prevent decay in wood and, as a result, tree paints fell out of favor. Recent studies indicate that while tree paints do not prevent internal wood decay, certain materials such as orange shellac may provide a temporary barrier to bark pathogens until a tree's natural barrier zones form. While the benefits of wound dressings continue to be debated by tree care professionals, most agree that conventional dressing materials are not injurious. Thus, they may be used at the discretion of whoever directs the work.

Begin the pruning of a tree at the time of planting. For balled-and-burlapped or containerized trees, some research has shown that post-planting growth is more rapid if pruning at planting time is limited to removing weak, dead, diseased, rubbing, or injured branches. Other tree experts still feel that for bare-root trees, approximately one-quarter of the crown should be thinned out at planting time to establish a new balance between the smaller root system and the crown.

The training of young trees normally begins one year after planting. Two general concepts that should guide the pruner are: 1) that the training can take place progressively over the course of three to five years, and 2) that no more pruning should take place in a single year than is needed to enhance the shape or structural strength of the tree.

In training a young tree, the first objective is to identify those primary limbs that will make up the tree's framework, the scaffold limbs. The height to the lowest scaffold limb will be determined partly by the anticipated activities under the tree. Will people play or mow beneath it, or will the tree be viewed from a distance? Often, it is possible to leave temporary scaffold limbs on the tree at lower heights than eventually will be desired. These will help to shade the thin bark on the young tree and provide additional leaf area and stems for producing and storing carbohydrates.

The scaffold branches selected should have wide angles of attachment with the trunk and should also be spaced approximately evenly from one another. This arrangement will provide the most structurally reliable connections between the branches and the trunk (Fig. 6).

Scaffold branches should also be distributed radially around the trunk; that is, the scaffolds should look like ascending spokes around a central axle (Fig. 7). This will provide a structurally strong tree that is attractive, balanced, and allows sunlight to penetrate and wind to pass through the canopy. Do not let one limb remain directly over a lower limb, causing it to be shaded out. One limb of such a pair should be removed.

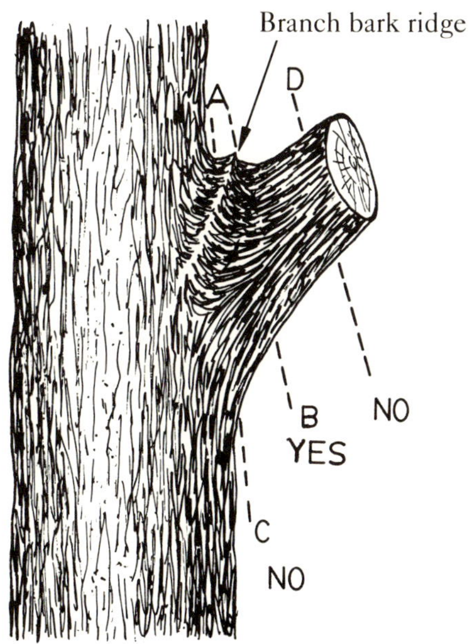

Figure 5. Proper location of pruning cut at branch collar (courtesy of Alex L. Shigo, "New Tree Health").

Unless the tree you are training naturally has a multi-stemmed habit, train the tree to a single leader. The terminal leader is the topmost vertical stem extending

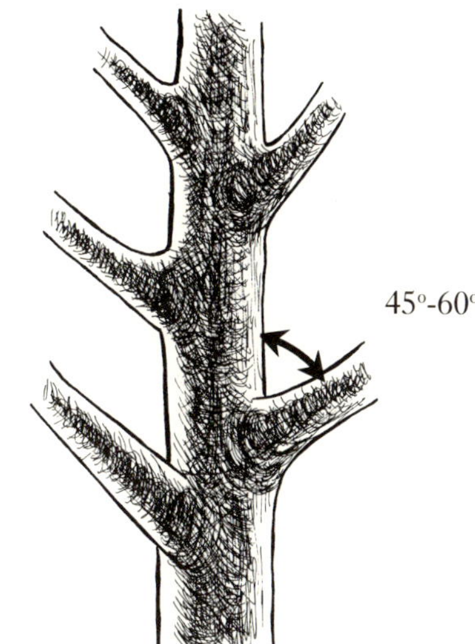

Figure 6. Optimum attachment of scaffold branches.

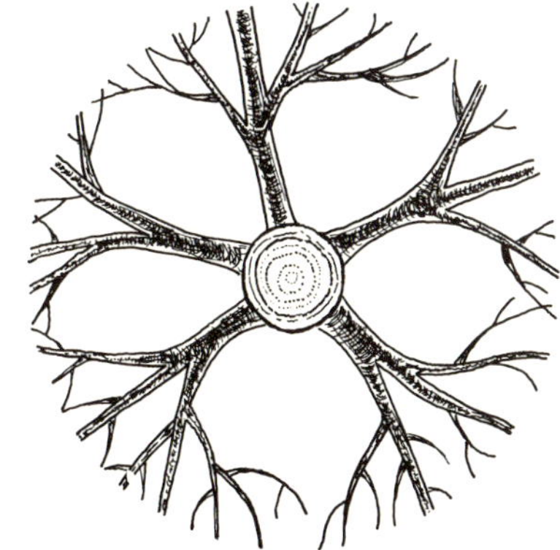

Figure 7. Radial arrangement of scaffold branches.

from the trunk. To be certain that this leader will remain dominant, prevent any laterals from growing higher than its tip.

In some cases, a tree will form a pair of codominant stems. If the two stems are truly equal, a branch bark ridge will be evident between them (Fig. 8a). Either one of the two equal stems can be removed to establish dominance, but if one stem is beginning to overtake the other, the weaker stem should be removed (Fig. 8b).

Once the scaffold system has been established, you may choose to alter the natural growth habit. For a tall, graceful tree that can be walked under, cut off all branches to a height of 7–8 feet once the tree is tall enough to retain three to four scaffold limbs above this height (Fig. 9).

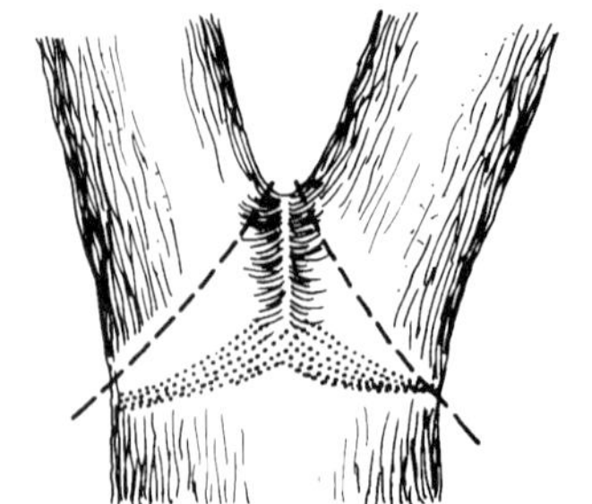

Figure 8a. Two equal codominant stems.

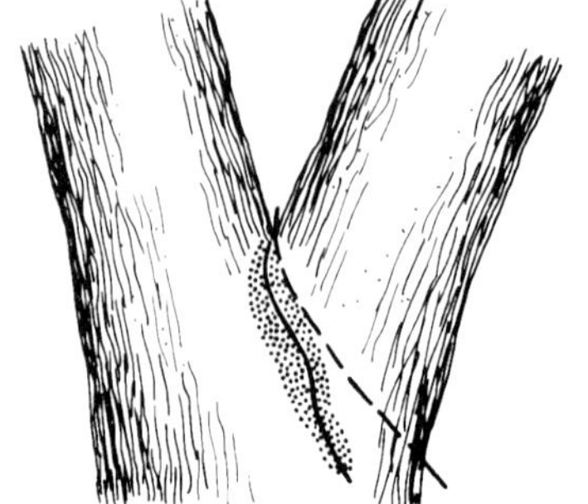

Figure 8b. Pruning to remove the weaker of two codominant stems. (Jim Houghton)

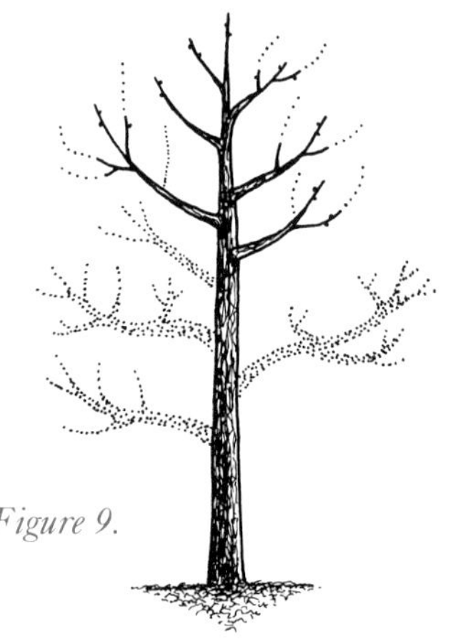

Figure 9.

As training continues in subsequent years, there are other practices that will encourage a healthy, long-lasting tree. Laterals that have grown higher than the terminal leader or beyond the perimeter of the crown should be pruned back to the bounds of the rest of the tree (Figs. 10a, b). Any laterals that have grown inward toward the center of the crown should probably be removed back to their origin. Water sprouts or suckers that frequently result from extensive pruning also should be removed because they are structurally weak and lead to overly dense growth in the interior of the crown, and can alter the natural growth habit of the tree (Figs. 11a, b).

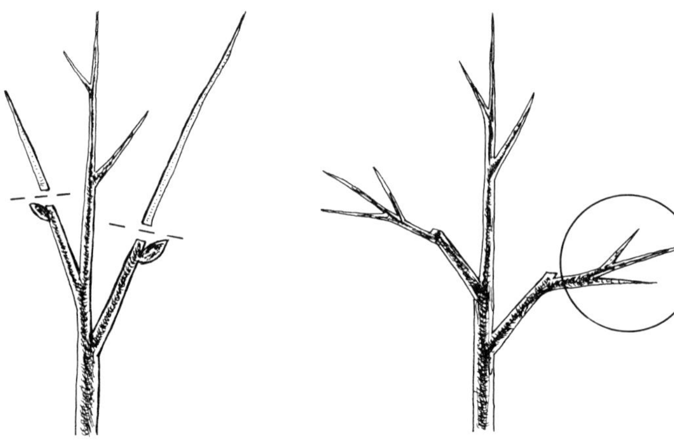

Figure 10a. Pruning back laterals that have grown taller than terminal leader.

Figure 10b. Growth resulting at season's end from pruning vigorous laterals.

Figure 11a.

Figure 11b.

Whenever removing a limb with a diameter exceeding 1 inch, use a three-cut method to avoid tearing the bark. Make the first cut with a handsaw or chain saw on the underside of the limb, 1-2 feet from the trunk, cutting half-way through the limb. The second cut is made on the top of the limb, 1 inch further out. As this cut is made, the limb's weight will cause it to break at the pivot point between the two cuts. Finish the job by making a clean cut with the saw along the branch bark ridge as described earlier. If the limb being removed is dead, it is likely that a collar of live wood has formed around it. Make the final cut just outside this live collar (Figs. 12a, b).

Even when all of the proper pruning practices are followed, the terminal leader can still be lost as a result of storms or insect or disease attacks. To train a new leader, select the topmost lateral on the highest scaffold, and prune off laterals that are immediately below it. This new leader can be forced into a vertical position by attaching it to a splint secured to the trunk below. After one full growing season, the wire or splint should be removed and the leader will stay permanently upright (Fig. 13).

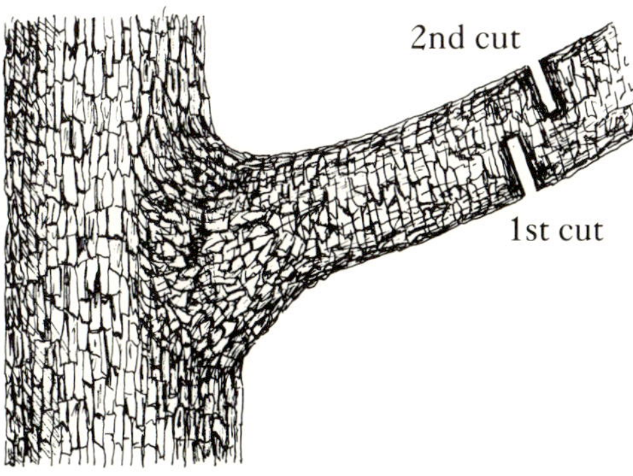

Figure 12a. Location of first and second cuts for pruning a limb exceeding 1 inch in diameter.

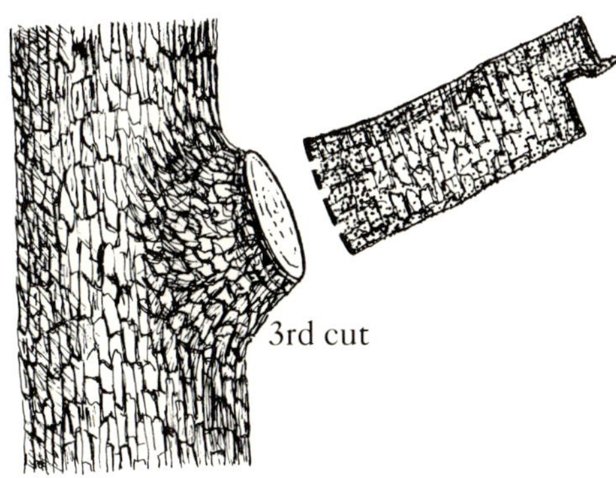

Figure 12b. Location of third cut.

As a tree matures, the number of scaffold limbs will increase. Eventually, the lowest scaffolds probably will need to be pruned away as they die, or when their drooping habit interferes with lawn activities. Although this practice is a natural part of tree maintenance, the tree will remain healthier if crown lifting (the removal of a large number of lower limbs at one time) is avoided.

Heavily branched tree species change as they mature in that the interior of the crown becomes increasingly shaded. Crown thinning will open up the interior canopy to make the foliage more productive and the tree more resistant to wind damage. It is advised that this practice be left to a professional arborist who would employ the National Arborist Association Pruning Standards.

The intended result of crown thinning is a tree with a more open habit that maintains its natural appearance. The first branches to remove in crown thinning are those that normally would be pruned away as part of a general clean-out: those that are dead, broken, weak, crossing, or diseased. This is followed by selective removal of limbs from the perimeter of the canopy, especially those growing closely together, or beyond the

Figure 13. Pruning and use of a splint to train a replacement leader. (Mary L. Westring)

Figure 14. Prune back branch to a lateral at least one-third diameter of the branch being removed.

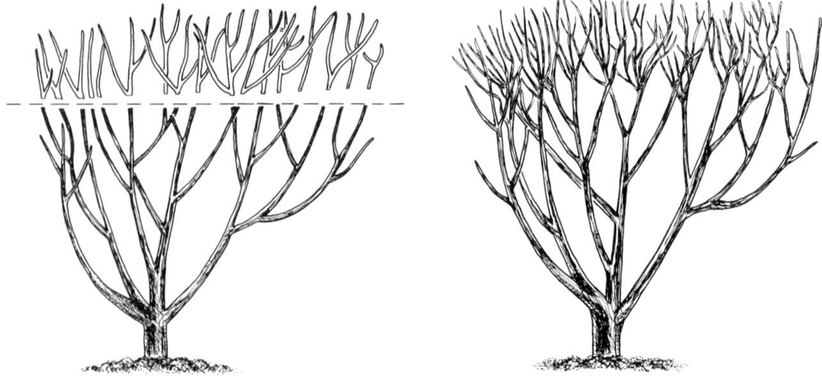

Figure 15a. *Figure 15b.*

Topping is a pruning procedure that should ***not*** *be followed.*

desired size of the crown, or with very narrow angles of attachment.

Any branches that are removed in the thinning out process should be taken back to their point of origin. Alternately, they can be pruned back to laterals that are at least one-third the diameter of the limb being removed (Fig. 14). This practice is called drop crotch pruning. Through these practices, subsequent water sprout development will be minimized and the desired natural appearance will be achieved. Open-branched species such as black walnut or Amur cork tree, or any evergreen species, such as pines and spruces, should never need crown thinning.

While thinning out is an accepted practice for reducing crown density and size, topping of the crown is not. In such pruning, main branches are cut back to stubs at a uniform height. This often-used technique is no longer recommended because resulting stubs can serve as entry points for decay fungi, and buds below the stubs are stimulated to grow, resulting in a profusion of water sprouts. Water sprouts cast a dense shade on the interior of the canopy, are structurally weak and thus prone to breakage, and they destroy the natural beauty of the tree (Figs. 15a, b). Topping should be limited to compact hedges, not inflicted on trees.

Pruning Evergreen Trees

Pruning evergreen trees, or conifers, involves somewhat different practices from those used on deciduous shade trees. When we think of conifers, we picture their beautiful conical shapes. They possess such shapes because each has a strong central leader that rarely is overcome by laterals from below. Because of this, and since young trees are normally heavily sheared by nursery operators, conifers typically need little training-type pruning in their early years in the landscape.

Conifers can be grouped on the basis of whether they have whorled branches, like pines, spruces, firs, and Douglas fir (Fig. 16); or random-branching patterns like arborvitae, cedar, *Chamaecyparis*, yew, and juniper (Fig. 17). In whorl-branched species, annual growth is determined by the number of shoots that are 'preformed' in the buds. Thus, there is normally just one flush of growth each year, and these preformed initials expand into stems and together form the whorl.

Pines can be made denser by pinching back the new-growth 'candles' 50 percent as they expand in the spring (Fig. 18). These new candles should be pinched by hand, since pruning with shears will cut the expanding needles and leave them with brown tips. Other whorl-branched conifers may also be pinched in the late spring (before new growth has matured) to promote greater density (Figs. 19a, b).

If a whorl-branched conifer has become too large, it can be pruned back only to active (needled) lateral shoots. Do not prune into the inactive central zone of conifers, since new tissue will not form to cover the remaining stubs.

Random-branched species can be subdivided into a yew group and an arborvitae, juniper, *Chamaecyparis*, and cedar group. *Taxus* (yews) contain latent growth points in the unneedled portions of the branches. These buds will generate new growth when pruning cuts are made just beyond them (see Fig. 28, page 17). Plants of the latter group do not have such latent buds and should be pruned only within the needled portions of the branches.

To reduce the overall size of random-branched conifers, try pruning just before bud break so that the new growth can mask pruning wounds. Maintenance trimming can be performed in summer to keep plants in the desired size range.

Figure 16. Pine species exhibiting typical whorled growth habit.

Figure 17. Typical random-branched conifer. (Theresa E. Jancek)

Figure 18. Pinch back new growth 50 percent on pines.

Figure 19a. New spring growth on spruce branch.

Figure 19b. Pinch back new growth 50 percent on spruce and other whorl-branched conifers.

Pruning Deciduous Shrubs

Maintenance

Deciduous shrubs require different degrees of maintenance pruning to keep them healthy and in scale with their surroundings. This type of pruning should commence at planting or after rejuvenating overgrown shrubs.

One aspect of maintenance work is thinning, the selective removal of branches to the base to keep the crown open. This practice should maintain the natural growth habit of the plant, but not cause an over-stimulation of growth. By maximizing light penetration, the shrub may be kept fully leafed throughout (Fig. 20).

Heading back, a second practice, involves cutting to the point of attachment with another outward facing branch or bud. Some careful heading back may be needed to keep the plant in size and character with its surroundings. Cleanup of shrubs includes the removal of unproductive, crossing, diseased, or broken branches, and should be pursued as needed.

Never shear shrubs, as this causes dense growth to form at the branch tips, in addition to creating an unnatural form. The exception to this is when the plant's intended use is in a hedge or other type of sculptured form.

The frequency of maintenance pruning depends on the shrub in question: perhaps annually with forsythia, but only once every 5-6 years with such slow-growing species as viburnum and witch hazel *(Hamamelis)*. Pruning can be done to excess, resulting in a loss of flowers and fruit formation. Prune only when there is a definite reason. By thinning out the oldest branches and heading back tall, leggy stems, most deciduous shrubs can be maintained at the proper height and spread for many years.

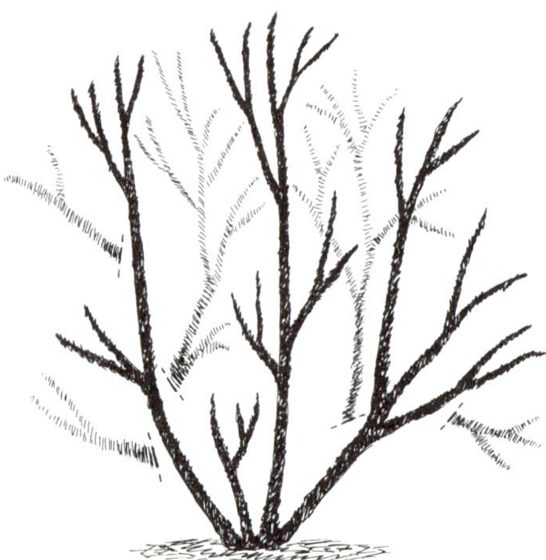

Figure 20. Selective thinning and heading back of branches on deciduous shrub.

Rejuvenation

Frequently, older shrubs become overly large for their surroundings, and have considerable amounts of unproductive wood. If they still have sufficient vigor and are growing in a location with adequate sunlight, they will respond to rejuvenation by one of several methods. This can be a drastic technique, however, and certain considerations must be kept in mind:

1. Proper timing; just before bud break in early spring is most preferred.
2. The negative effect on the plant's food-making potential (photosynthetic surface area).
3. The importance of after-care (fertilization, watering, pest control.)
4. The immediate impact on the landscape at the time of pruning.

Depending on the method selected, it may take 2-4 years to achieve the desired results.

Method 1. Severing at base of crown is the simplest procedure for handling seriously overgrown shrubs. This one-step process involves cutting the entire plant back to the base, or within 6-10 inches of the ground (Fig. 21a).

An excessive number of new, upright canes will develop from the base by early to midsummer, producing a porcupine-like appearance. Once the canes have reached their fullest elongation (July), half or more of them must be removed and some of those remaining headed back (Fig. 21b). The height of the canes should vary, but all should be well below the desired final size of the shrub to encourage low branching.

Prune back to outward-pointing buds, so that the inner portion of the plant does not become overly dense. This will result in good light transmission into the shrub, encouraging proper growth development. In cases where the spurt of cane growth is truly excessive, or developing canes quickly grow overly long and succulent, it may be advisable to root prune the shrub to slow the vigor.

Method 2. Overall unequal height at one pruning is also a one-shot approach, but less drastic than the previously described technique. Instead of clean-cutting, 50 percent or more of the branches are selected for removal at the base. These would include all older, unproductive wood, inward-growing branches, and any other growth that detracts from the natural form of the plant. Any extremely vigorous, unbranched suckers also should be removed at their point of origin (Figs. 22a, b).

As this project nears completion, examine for any remaining out-of-place branches. Head these back further to outward-facing lateral branches or buds.

By midsummer, new shoots will have developed, both from existing branches as well as from the crown. Many of these new basal canes should be removed at this time. For continued management of the plant, consult the Maintenance pruning section on page 12.

Method 3. Multi-year sequence, a still less-drastic course of action, involves annual removal of one-quarter to one-third of the oldest, unproductive branches over a period of 3-4 years (Figs. 23a, b). Obviously, it takes a concerted effort to return annually until the job is complete, but the shrub remains more attractive throughout the rejuvenation period. At completion, all old wood will have been replaced by young, productive growth. This procedure probably will also stimulate excessive canes, both from the crown and on the remaining branches of the plant. This new growth should be selectively removed and headed back as described in Method 1.

Figure 21a. Rejuvenation by severing stems at the base.

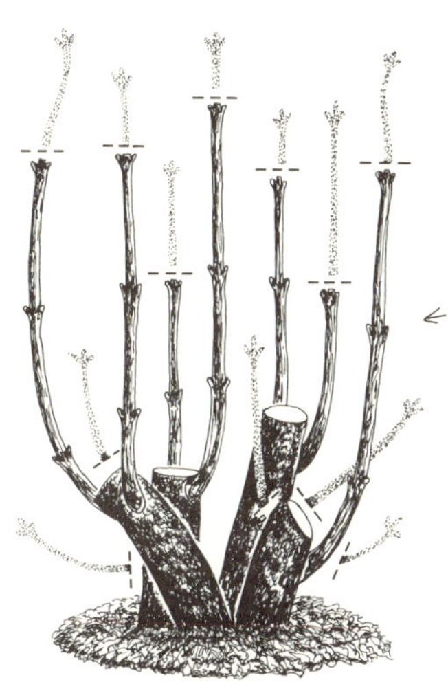

Figure 21b. Heading back and removing new canes.

Figure 22a.

Figure 22b.

Figure 23a. One-quarter to one-third of oldest, nonproductive branches are removed each year.

Figure 23b. Effect of first-year pruning in multi-year sequence of rejuvenation.

Pruning Evergreen Shrubs

Broad-leaved evergreens

Maintenance

Most broad-leaved evergreens, such as rhododendrons (including evergreen azalea), andromeda, evergreen barberry, boxwood, and holly, require limited amounts of pruning on a very selective basis. This could be undertaken to improve or enhance the natural habit of the bush and/or to keep it in scale with its surroundings. In addition, such pruning can promote fuller new growth from within the crown. Generally, this work can be done whenever convenient for the gardener. For the least sacrifice of bloom, prune shortly after flowering but before the next year's flower buds are set in July. Cut back any out-of-place branches to a lateral or, if heading back a young vigorous cane, be sure to cut above a few remaining leaves.

Tradition states that 'deadheading' can be practiced with truss-forming broad-leaved evergreens such as rhododendron and mountain laurel. Experts differ on the importance of this chore. Some claim that seed capsules allowed to develop do not appreciably affect flower and shoot development for the coming year ("It doesn't occur in nature!"). Others feel that deadheading will result in a fuller shrub with better quality blooms.

If you do plan to deadhead, simply snap out the faded flower truss with your fingers, while holding the branch with your other hand (Figs. 24a, b). This must be accomplished as soon as the flowers begin to fade. Use care to avoid damaging the vegetative buds or new shoots that form directly below the flower heads.

Rejuvenation

Broad-leaved evergreens sometimes get too large and/or leggy for their location. All healthy broad-leaved evergreen shrubs can be successfully rejuvenated if the procedure is carried out in late winter or early spring before growth begins. This may be considered drastic pruning by the novice gardener, but it is perfectly acceptable in the appropriate circumstances. A similar action occurs in nature when fire destroys the tops of rhododendrons or mountain laurel, and new shoots arise from the base to form a new compact plant.

Different techniques in rejuvenating broad-leaved evergreens are possible:

1) Sever at the base of the crown; full rejuvenation will take 2–4 years. (Appropriate for rhododendrons, boxwood, and cherry laurel [Figs. 25a, b].)

2) For multi-stemmed plants, completely remove a few of the oldest trunks each year for a period of 2–3 years. This approach works very well for *Leucothoe*, and evergreen barberry.

3) Overgrown shrubs that may require some height reduction into bare, leafless wood (e.g., mountain laurel, evergreen hollies) can be pruned at varying heights of 2–4 feet from the ground. This form of rejuvenation must be done in early spring and all at one time. By cutting at varying heights, the developing vegetative shoots will not appear uniform. The plant will then reestablish its natural habit of growth.

Special care is important for any plant that has been drastically pruned. If rejuvenation is the anticipated goal, fertilize the plant in question the fall prior to spring pruning. Otherwise, make the application immediately following pruning. The ability of the plant to produce ample new and healthy growth hinges on this and other proper horticultural procedures: watering, mulching, and insect and disease control.

Pyracantha, or fire thorn, is an exception to the pruning procedures described above in that it requires a greater degree and frequency of pruning to avoid becoming an unmanageable size. Determining the best time for annual pruning is difficult since the next year's flowers (and fruit) are produced on the previous season's wood (Fig. 26). If too much wood is removed each year, the plant will be left with few of the colorful fruit so essential to the beauty of this shrub. In late winter or early spring, select for removal only those branches most out of scale. This will allow enough of the previous season's growth to remain to assure adequate flowering. If the plant is excessively overgrown, there is little choice but to rejuvenate in late winter or early spring. Since this practice will eliminate nearly all flowers for the next spring, it is more desirable to prune selectively each year, rather than heavily every several years.

Heaths and Heathers

Among the heaths, *Erica carnea* is the only reliably hardy species in most parts of the Northeast. Although this species responds well to pruning, no regular pruning routine is required if plants have room to grow and receive sufficient sunlight. If plants need to be reduced in size, prune any time between end of bloom (usually early May) and the first week of July. Flowering the following spring will not be affected.

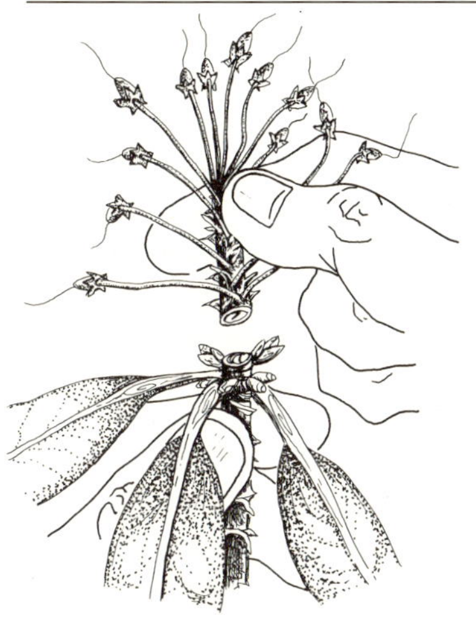

Figure 24a. Deadheading by snapping out the faded flower trusses.

Figure 24b. One year after deadheading.

Figure 25a. Basal zone for pruning broad-leaved evergreen shrub for rejuvenation.

Figure 25b. Severing broad-leaved evergreen shrub at base of crown.

In addition to selecting an appropriate planting site, one hard annual pruning (crew-cutting) is a key factor in maintaining healthy plants of heather *(Calluna)*. They respond well by forcing new growth from hidden buds. In the Northeast, in contrast to England or Oregon, this pruning is best done following winter, but before spring growth commences (early April–mid-May). Flowers develop on the new wood, with most varieties blooming in July-August. If the wood is badly damaged from desiccation the previous winter, cut until the green rings of live cambium are evident, even if the foliage is lost.

In many landscapes, situations may exist where a tightly sheared, geometric shrub is desired. Because of their thicket-type growth, this type of treatment is often considered for evergreen azaleas. Although they will usually respond to such pruning because latent buds exist far along the branches, this technique is better used on other evergreens. Azaleas naturally exhibit an attractive growth habit that should not be mutilated. When tightly sheared, flowers appear only at the branch tips.

Figure 26. Pruning of a Pyracantha (fire thorn).

Narrow-leaved evergreens

Maintenance

Of foremost importance with narrow-leaved evergreen plants is knowing what you have or intend to purchase. Far too many narrow-leaved evergreens initially look like shrubs but quickly outgrow their surroundings, ultimately becoming trees! Hemlock and certain *Chamaecyparis*, juniper, and arborvitae species are not meant for foundation planting. Use of hedge shears will prove futile in any attempt to keep them in bounds. Though not readily apparent, sheared shrubs continue to enlarge in size. With repeated tight shearing, very dense needle growth develops at the tips, decreasing light penetration to the inner part of the plant. This results in excessive inner needle drop and hinders natural renewal growth from within the plant.

Maintenance pruning is done to enhance the natural form and habit of the plant, and to keep its growth controlled and open for good light penetration. Timing of selective pruning is less critical for coniferous evergreens because they are not included in the landscape for their flowering ability. Whether they are pruned in early spring before growth commences, or during the winter holidays for decorative use of the 'greens' or as a winter mulch, makes little difference. A second light thinning and heading back of new growth should be performed in late June to early July.

Thinning is generally done every year to prevent a plant from getting overly large. On Japanese yews, junipers, and other spreading evergreens, it involves the pruning of longer, out-of-scale branches to a point back within the plant—either to an inner lateral or to just above vigorous side shoots on the two- or three-year-old wood. Start the process at the top and work down, removing those branches that extend out and over lower shorter ones below. This allows the lower branches proper exposure to light. Do not cut back all branches to the same length, otherwise the intended natural habit of the plant will be destroyed. By making pruning cuts so that they are hidden by part of an overlapping branch, there will be no indication that the shrub was pruned. Remember to keep the diameter of the top of the plant smaller than that of the base.

Ground-cover type conifers, like creeping junipers and *Microbiota*, may also require trimming near a walk, border, or edging. Do not shear, but cut back branches at varying distances to preserve the natural look (Fig. 27).

Mugo pine is generally considered a dwarf conifer, but still may require annual pruning to keep its compact form. This is accomplished by nipping the new candles back by about 50 percent when the shoots have fully elongated and are still soft.

Figure 27. Recommended pruning of spreading evergreens.

Rejuvenation

Most narrow-leaved evergreens do not have adventitious buds on old wood, as do the broad-leaved forms. Thus, mature overgrown plants of *Chamaecyparis*, juniper, hemlock, and others cannot be topped or cut back into old needleless wood without mutilating them. The voids caused by heavy interior pruning will not be filled in by new growth. Once these plants become too large for their existing location, it's best to remove them, or possibly, prune up the lower branches, allowing the plant to develop as an open, multi-trunked tree form.

There are, however, a few exceptions to the above rule. *Taxus* (yews) and, in some instances, arborvitae have the ability to initiate new growth from old woody inner branches. These plants can be cut back severely into needleless wood and will rejuvenate new growth (Fig. 28). As mentioned earlier under broad-leaved evergreens, this procedure must be done in early spring and to healthy plants. Prune branches back to irregular heights so that the result is a return of the plant to a natural growth habit.

Figure 28. Magnified view, one year after cutting back into needleless wood to rejuvenate new growth.

Figure 29a A multi-stemmed shrub may be converted to a small tree.

Figure 29b. Single-stem small tree from shrub.

Manipulating Shrubs into Small Trees

A unique aspect of pruning involves the training of shrubs into small trees. This can occur in two forms, multi-stemmed or single trunk. Practice the former with a large overgrown shrub in the mature landscape, as well as with a young shrub as it is developing. To train a shrub into a single-stemmed small tree, the procedure must be initiated very early in the plant's life to insure a properly formed central leader and upright branching structure.

Many large-growing shrubs lend themselves to one or both of these processes. A mature mountain laurel can be given this honor—three or five stems pruned to expose interesting twisting growth and a picturesque upper crown. While attaining a height of 6-10 feet, a mountain laurel can be an extremely interesting addition to the landscape as a small tree. Other appropriate shrubs to consider for large multiple-branched trees are *Syringa vulgaris* (common lilac), *Lonicera maackii* (Amur honeysuckle), *Hamamelis virginiana* (native witch hazel), and *Viburnum plicatum* var. tomentosum (doublefile viburnum)(Fig. 29a).

When training a small shrub for single-stem development, it is often necessary to stake the trunk for a year or two to insure good vertical symmetry and support of the upper crown. Shrubs that make good candidates for adaptation to small, single-stemmed trees include *Viburnum prunifolium* (black haw), *V. sieboldii*, *Cornus racemosa* (gray dogwood), *Euonymus europaea* (spindle tree), *Photinia villosa*, *Rhus copallina* (shining sumac), *R. typhina*, and *Syringa reticulata* (Japanese tree lilac) (Fig. 29b). Bear in mind, these single-stemmed trees will ultimately attain heights of 15–25 feet. They are small specimens in the right location. Do not expect them to develop into grandiose, large trees; they lack the genetic potential to do so.

This adaptation from a normal shrub cannot be carried out without follow-up and periodic maintenance. Some plants more than others must be kept under control by careful selective pruning to reduce spread, assure a picturesque open habit, and emphasize the larger stems and trunks. The result is a plant that can stand alone, whether grown more naturally as a large 3- or 4-stemmed tree-like shrub or to a single trunk.

Hedges

Hedges have many functions. They do not occur naturally, but when used and trained properly, can be appealing and can effectively blend with existing surroundings. If you shave the sides and give them a 'crew-cut' on top, you will have a formal hedge. Permit them to grow more irregularly, and the result will be a more naturalistic screen. A properly maintained hedge requires skill and dedication to keep it in good repair and appearance.

It is imperative to begin intensive pruning at the time of planting. If gaps in the bottom of a hedge are to be avoided, pruning must be started early so that the top width is narrower than the bottom. This permits sunlight to reach the lower foliage as well as that near the top. With some evergreen and all deciduous shrubs, cut plants back (both sides and top) by about one-third. This first cut determines the future density of the hedge. In addition to the outward-facing portions (front and back) of each shrub, the right and left sides of every plant should receive an initial first-year trimming. Although this sacrifices one year of initial growth, by trimming all sides to eliminate any loose interlocking branches, each succeeding year's growth will develop uniformly throughout the hedge.

Follow-up pruning of the established hedge depends on the degree of formality and, to some extent, the type of plant used for the hedge. The possibilities are many. (It is unfortunate that only about six different genera of plants get constant use.) Certain types of shrubs and trees make better formal hedges (*Taxus,* California privet, Korean boxwood, hawthorn, beech, Amur and hedge maples); others are better adapted to the informal, natural look (arborvitae, hemlock, alpine currant, and certain spireas). The former are sheared, the latter are selectively pruned. Both techniques must be done with care.

The formal hedge generally requires more frequent shearing (1-3 times per year, depending on the plant used). When the hedge is pruned for a formal look (Fig. 30a), new shoots that persist for any duration will make it appear unkempt. Major shearing is accomplished shortly after the main flush of spring growth has fully elongated in early July. Follow-up shearing is done as necessary. Informal hedges are cut once or twice yearly; a major pruning is done in late winter or early spring, with a follow-up in July when necessary. Informal hedges, although set in rows, should be allowed to grow somewhat freely, following their natural growth habit and yet conforming to some planned regularity of line (Fig. 30b).

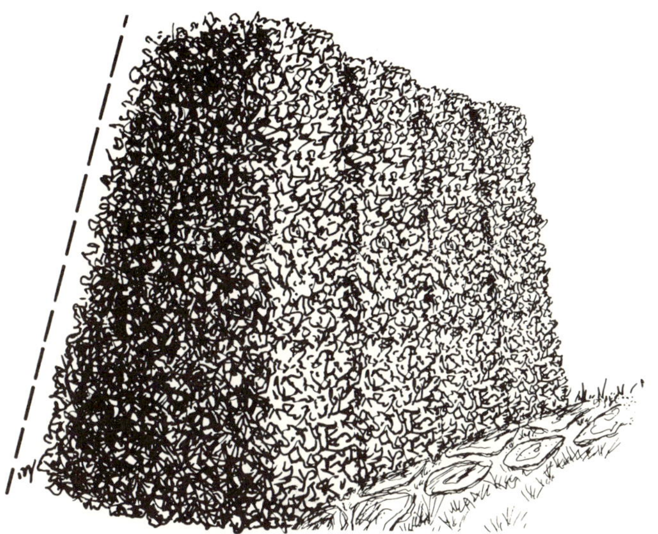

Figure 30a. A formal hedge. (Theresa E. Jancek)

Figure 30b. An informal hedge.

If a formal hedge is being rejuvenated or requires corrective leveling, string a taut line to guide cutting at the desired height. Taking the time to assure equal dimensions throughout the hedge will be rewarded at each successive shearing. To permit the clippings to fall more easily from the top, shear the sides first. Once the proper width has been established, the trimmer will have a far better sense of the desired height to cut. As for any type of pruning, the shears and/or hedge clippers must be properly selected and kept sharp, or the many cut surfaces will look ragged and heal slowly.

Figure 31. English ivy exhibiting climbing tendrils ('holdfasts').

Figure 32. Clematis vine exhibiting typical twining growth habit.

Vines

Vines have a very definite place in the landscape. They should be used with far greater frequency, both for their aesthetic value and function. It must be understood, however, that vines do require appropriate pruning on a regular basis if they are to remain within the desired scale of their surroundings. Once a vine becomes unmanageable and unsightly, special skill and extra effort may be necessary to bring it back into proper balance. By having a clear picture of a vine's function in the landscape, pruning can be carried out in accordance with your needs and the plant's growth habit. Generally, frequent light thinning will increase a vine's density. Vigorously growing vines that are periodically cut back to the ground and thinned will be less dense.

The major reasons for routine pruning of vines include limiting vigorous growth, clearing around windows and doors, enhancement of flowering, thinning branches, and removal of unproductive, dead, or damaged wood. Prune most vines annually and while they are in a dormant condition. Viewing the leafless structure of a deciduous vine makes the pruning process much easier and desired growth has the entire next growing season to develop and mature.

Vines climb by different means and this can determine the type and amount of pruning they require. Those that are self-clinging and secured by 'holdfasts' (for example, Virginia creeper, Boston and English ivies, climbing hydrangea) require very little pruning other than removal of dead wood and trimming the new growth where it is unwanted. If this type of vine is pulled off its support and partially cut back to the ground, do not attempt to retrain any remaining portion of the old vine. Once removed, 'holdfasts' lose their clinging ability (Fig. 31).

Twining vines, those that climb by means of coiling tendrils (this includes most other vines), initiate most of their growth from upper buds, often leaving the lower crown devoid of foliage (Fig. 32). In such cases, it may be necessary to cut the vine back severely to force initiation of a new lower top from latent basal buds. A mass of new shoots will appear. Select approximately one-third of the strongest and retrain them. When they have elongated to their desired length, head back to restrict them to their allotted area.

Whenever possible, remove old nonproductive shoots and those densely entangled or crossing. Train new shoots to fill the voids.

In certain cases, during the yearly flush of spring growth, vines develop an excessive number of elongated shoots with few lateral branches. Such vigorous growth may need further pruning during the growing season to encourage lateral branch development and horizontal spread.

To enhance the proper branch development of newly planted vines, provide careful initial pruning to encourage new growth at the base of the vine and increase the vigor of already-existing shoots. Select 3-5 of the strongest shoots, and cut these back by one-half. Many new shoots will appear following this initial pruning. Thin most of these, retaining only enough to fill in the voids.

Wisteria and Clematis

Wisteria is an extremely popular vine, sought after for its extraordinary bloom; but to guarantee profuse flowering and prevent excessive, unruly growth, it demands a special pruning schedule.

Never prune heavily during the dormant season; excessive vegetative growth will be encouraged the following spring. Late-summer or early fall pruning is most important for flower bud initiation on the pruned-back lateral shoots. Reduce the spur-bearing shoot length by one-half or greater, leaving about 6 nodes (Fig. 33). The result will be short flowering spurs where next year's flowers will be borne. Any excessively vigorous vegetative shoots can be either removed entirely or trained to fill a void in the overall framework.

Follow-up pruning to further shorten the spur growth can be done in winter or very early spring. Cut back to about 3 plump flower buds per spur (Fig. 34). At this time, it is easy to differentiate between them and the flat vegetative buds.

Clematis species also require special pruning, based on when a particular species blooms: those that bloom on current season's wood *(Clematis jackmani, C. paniculata, C. tangutica,* and *C. viticella),* and those flowering on one-year-old wood *(C. florida, C. patens, C. montana,* and *C. alpina).* The former can be pruned ruthlessly in late winter or early spring to promote new growth from the lowest 2-3 feet of growth (Fig. 35). Prune shoots at different heights to extend the floral coverage and period of bloom. The latter group should be sparingly pruned (removing only dead and weak wood and straggling branches) soon after flowering (Fig. 36). After five or more years, varieties that flower on old wood may get too tall and leggy. In such cases, severe cutting back is beneficial, even though the current

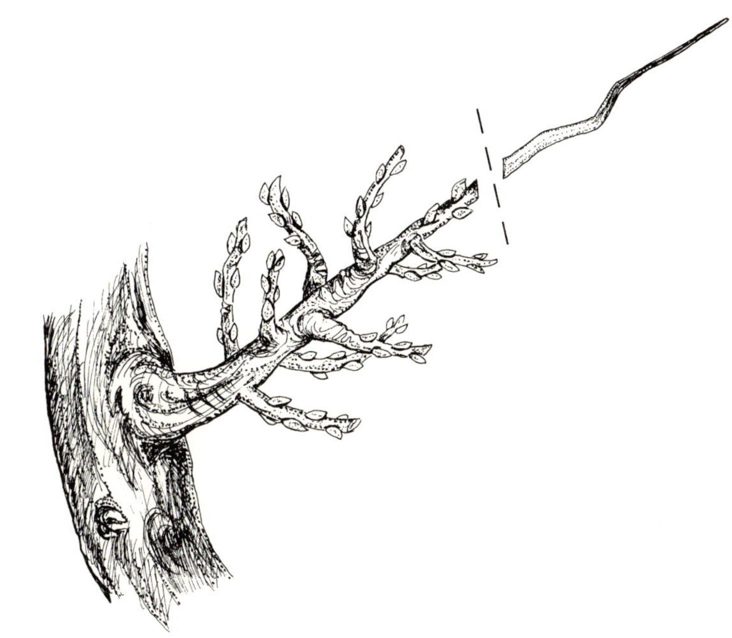

Figure 33. Pruned wisteria shoot with 6-7 spurs remaining.

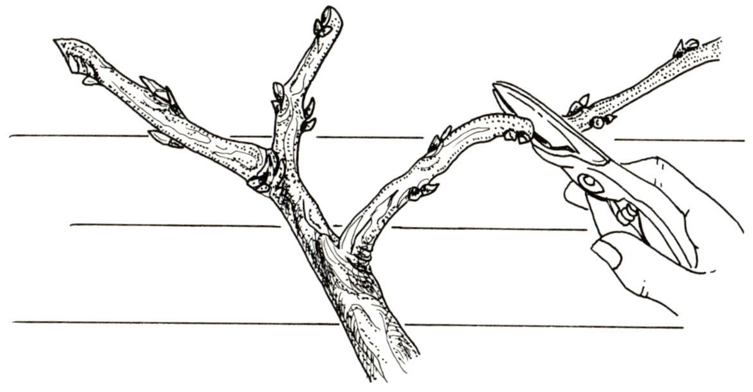

Figure 34. Spurs pruned back to 3 flower buds.

Figure 35. A clematis species that blooms on current season's wood, pruned back severely in late winter.

Figure 36. Clematis species that bloom on 1-year-old wood should be sparingly pruned.

year's bloom will be sacrificed. If newly planted, regardless of classification, cut back at once to the lowest pair of strong buds. This will induce additional growth from the crown.

Topiary, Pollarding, and Espalier

These three specialized pruning techniques are appropriate for certain plants in some situations. None of them provides a natural appearance to plants. Thus, all require a diligent pruning schedule to maintain the special forms.

Topiary

This type of pruning or art form involves the training and shearing of plants to grow in unnatural shapes such as animals, squares, spirals, cylinders, or "poodles." Occasionally these work effectively in formal settings or park-like areas where they can be featured accents, but are generally not very compatible with existing plants in the residential landscape. The increasingly common "poodled" juniper that is planted in a key location in so many newer suburban landscapes can be quite an eyesore. These forms look totally out of place as specimens and will shortly become trimming nightmares!

If one has a sincere interest in this practice, patience and skill are required to keep topiary shapes maintained. It takes time to achieve good specimens: 4-5 years for simpler shapes, 10-20 years for the elaborate. Initial training requires controlled tying of branches and twigs to a temporary form until they remain in their desired position. Shearing continues during the development process and throughout the life of the plant.

To some it's a fad; to others it's a love. "If you like that sort of foolishness," as Disraeli once said, "that's the sort of foolishness you like."

Pollarding

This procedure is similar to topping (see page 10), but is initiated as the tree is developing, and is repeated every year. The result is a formal appearance and keeps large growing trees confined. With pollarded trees, a cut is made at the same location each time, and generally at the terminals of primary scaffold branches. After a tree has been pollarded for several years, a knob of branch stubs and bark callus develops at the end of each stem. Fast-growing trees planted in difficult locations are most often used for this practice, for example, London plane, linden, catalpa, and mulberry.

Espalier

This atypical technique involves the training of certain trees and shrubs so that the branches lie in one plane. Branches are supported on taut wires or a trellis, fence, or pipe that is usually installed against a wall, or may be freestanding.

Recently, espalier plants have regained some popularity. For centuries, fruit trees were the principal plants used for espalier work. The technique requires little space in small garden plots, and blooming and fruit maturity are hastened by heat reflected from walls facing the sun. The current resurgence of espalier is linked to those architectural styles that are enhanced by this plant form. Homes with large expanses of windowless walls require some ornamentation. A carefully chosen espalier can provide an artistic touch through the design and manipulation achieved by the plant's branches. Another possible reason for its increased popularity is the greater diversity of plants that can be effectively and easily espaliered. The choices are no longer limited to fruit trees, but include *Taxus* (yew), *Euonymus alatus,* many of the viburnums and cotoneasters, *Cornus kousa, Ilex crenata, Chaenomeles* species (flowering quince), forsythia, and magnolia. Flowering, fruiting, fall color, foliage texture, and/or branching structure all enter into the selection process.

The design patterns used for espalier work are usually of two distinctly different types, formal and informal(Figs. 37a, b). Whichever is selected, there is an endless array of design arrangements that can be created using one's imagination or by consulting texts on the subject. As one might assume, the formal approach is very precise and structured, requiring a higher degree of maintenance to look tidy. The informal style is not rigid, allowing the branches to grow more as nature might suggest. At the same time, the individual characteristics of the specimen plant are displayed to best advantage.

Anyone wishing to grow espaliered plants should be aware that: 1) the process can be time-consuming and require considerable skill, 2) training young plants (which is always advised) can be a slow process, and 3) care must be exercised in placing plants against south-facing walls because of reflected heat. Spacing the horizontal, vertical, and/or diagonal supports about 4-6 inches from the face of the wall or building is generally suggested to allow for good air circulation, branch development, and easier maintenance. Lastly, be aware of ready-made espaliers that are now popular features in retail nurseries and are used increasingly by designers and architects in their landscape projects. Although these plants are generally of excellent quality and ably satisfy their intended use, they will not maintain themselves and retain their stature without diligent, continued training and pruning.

Chemical Control of Growth

Although not a pruning technique per se, the application of growth-inhibiting chemicals is another way in which trees can be kept in a desired height range. Growth inhibitors are currently used most widely by utility companies for restricting tree growth under power lines. Among the materials that are currently used are paclobutrazol (Profile 2SC Tree Growth Regulator), uniconozol (Sumagic), and flurprimidol (Cutless). These products may be used only by certified commercial arborists. They should not be seen as a long-term solution to planting an inappropriate specimen in a particular site.

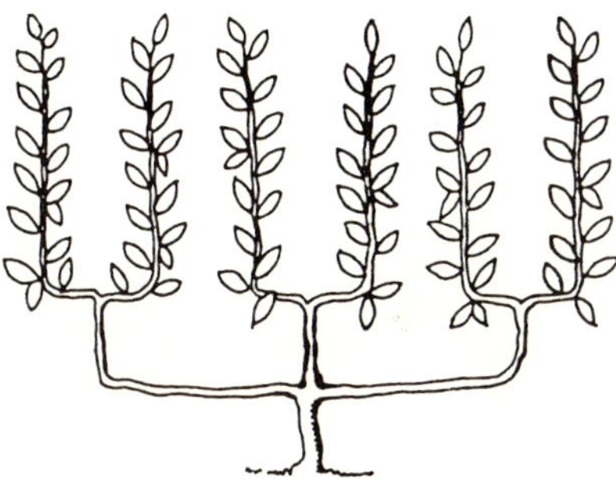

Figure 37a. A typical formal espalier design. (Univ. of Connecticut)

Figure 37b. A typical informal espalier design. (Univ. of Connecticut)

Seasonal Pruning Calendar

EARLY SPRING: just before bud break

- best time to prune roses and summer blooming shrubs: hydrangea, rose-of-Sharon, glossy abelia, *Buddleia* (butterfly bush), *Caryopteris* (bluebeard), *Cornus* (dogwood species with brightly colored bark), *Hypericum* (St.-John's-wort), *Perovskia* (Russian sage), privet, *Potentilla* (cinquefoil), *Sorbaria* (false spirea), *Spiraea bumalda*, *S. billiardii*, and *Symphoricarpos* (snowberry).
- head back growth of random-branched conifer species: junipers, *Chamaecyparis* (false cypress), yews, and arborvitae.
- train young shade trees planted the previous year by selecting scaffold branches, removing others.
- preferred time to rejuvenate evergreen and deciduous shrubs and hedges that are out of bounds.
- best time to annually prune most vines.
- alternate time to thin mature trees.
- avoid pruning species prone to bleeding (birch, elm, maple, yellowwood).

SPRING: bud break

- best not to prune any woody plants at this time due to translocation of carbohydrates and growth hormones to growing points.

SPRING/EARLY SUMMER: leaves fully expanded

- rub off trunk buds that will give rise to suckers and water sprouts.
- prune spring-flowering shrubs soon after blooming period: azaleas, *Deutzia*, pearlbush, *Forsythia*, *Kerria*, *Kolkwitzia* (beauty bush), ninebark, *Philadelphus* (mock orange), *Rhododendron*, *Spiraea prunifolia* (bridalwreath spirea), *S. thunbergii*, *S. vanhouttei*, and *Weigela*.
- for more compact growth, pinch out one-half of the new growth of pines, spruces, and firs.
- clip back the terminals of vigorous new shoots as well as spent flowers in ericaceous species (*Rhododendron*, azaleas, mountain laurel, andromeda); this will keep plants compact and encourage production of side shoots and flower buds.
- evergreen shrubs or hedges that were pruned heavily in late winter or early spring can be trimmed now to reestablish clean lines.

SUMMER: new shoots reach full growth and start to become woody.

- preferred time to perform major thinning operations on crab apples, callery pears, ornamental cherries and plums, honey locust, maples, spruces, willows, and poplars to reduce susceptibility to trunk cankers.
- rework the interiors of tree-form dogwoods to remove overly shaded, crisscrossed, or weak branches.
- alternate time to rejuvenate hedges.

LATE SUMMER: new shoots fully mature; early stages of fall color

- heavy pruning at this time can result in stimulation of new shoots that may not properly harden before winter; limit pruning to the removal of damaged or dead wood, especially on conifers.

EARLY FALL: full coloration of leaves; some leaf fall.

- wisteria may be pruned at this time.

LATE FALL: after several hard frosts

- clip away excess ivy growth on building walls and around windows: English ivy, Boston ivy, and Virginia creeper.
- alternate time to perform major pruning of noncanker-prone species.

WINTER: after hard freezes; plants truly dormant

- thin crowns of mature trees; remove dead or storm-damaged limbs.
- clip hedges to retain clean lines.
- in late winter rejuvenate shrubs that are out-of-bounds.

Glossary of Terms

adventitious buds: growth buds that appear in locations where they are not ordinarily expected; usually appear after an injury or pruning.

bleeding: the exuding of sap from wounds by certain species in early spring.

bonsai: the art of pruning and culture to produce miniature forms of trees.

branch bark ridge: a zone that forms where xylem tissue of the trunk meets that of the branch; a strong protective zone when pruning cuts are made.

callus: scar tissue made up of large, thin-walled cells that forms around wounds.

candle: the new expanding growth on pines.

compartmentalize: the process by which woody plants internally wall off a wound from healthy tissue.

crew-cutting: pruning a shrub back to a uniform height, at or near the ground level, as part of a rejuvenation process or as an annual maintenance activity (see Heaths and Heathers, p. 14).

crown thinning: reducing the number of shoots on a tree's branch system.

deadheading: removing the spent flowers or unripe seed pods from a plant such as a rhododendron.

decurrent: trees with round-headed habit and no main leader when mature.

desiccation: the drying and subsequent death of plant tissue, including leaves or portions thereof.

espalier: to train a tree to grow flat against a fence or wall, usually in a regular pattern.

excurrent: trees with a strong central leader and a cone-shaped crown when mature.

hardiness: the relative cold tolerance of woody plant tissue.

heading back: cutting back stems on a shrub, hedge, or vine to the point of attachment of another outward-facing branch or bud.

holdfast: a cup-shaped plant part by which certain vines cling to flat surfaces.

inflorescence: the flowering structure of a plant; may be solitary or in clusters.

latent bud: a bud that does not develop (open) in the season it was formed.

lateral: a branch attached to and subordinate to a scaffold branch.

leader: a developing terminal stem that is longer and more vigorous than any laterals.

lifting the crown: the removal of a large number of lower limbs at one time.

pinch back: pruning by cutting back the growing tip of a shoot using thumb and forefinger.

pollarding: the practice of pruning tree branches back to the same uniform points every year.

pruning: selective removal of specific parts of a plant for the benefit of the whole plant.

rejuvenation: pruning undertaken to restore overgrown shrubs to their former vigor and/or size.

remedial pruning: pruning to remove broken, dead, diseased, weak, or heavily shaded branches.

root pruning: the cutting or removal of some of a plant's roots; in conjunction with transplanting, to slow shoot growth after pruning, or to encourage flowering (wisteria).

scaffold branches: the primary limbs that form the structure of the canopy.

shearing: pruning method for removing excessive growth from shrubs and hedges; shearing produces a smooth, straight surface.

sucker: a vigorous shoot that originates from the roots, or trunk beneath the ground, or rootstock below the graft union.

topiary: shaping a tree or bush into a dense unnatural form, usually an animal or geometric shape.

topping: tree pruning practice in which the main branches are cut back to stubs at a uniform height.

truss: a flower cluster, usually growing at the terminal of a stem or branch (e.g., rhododendron).

vegetative growth: stem growth that does not directly lead to flower or fruit production.

water sprout: a vigorous upright shoot that originates along the branch, normally at the site of pruning.

whorl: circular growth of branches around the growing tip.

This information is presented with the understanding that no product discrimination is intended and no endorsement of any product mentioned or criticism of unnamed products are implied.

Cornell Cooperative Extension

Helping You Put Knowledge to Work

Additional copies of this publication may be purchased from Cornell University, Media and Technology Services Resource Center, 7 Cornell Business & Technology Park, Ithaca, NY 14850. Phone: 607-255-2080. Fax: 607-255-9946. E-mail: Dist_Center@cce.cornell.edu

A free catalog of Cornell Cooperative Extension publications and audiovisuals is available from the same address, or from any Cornell Cooperative Extension office. The catalog also can be accessed at the following World Wide Web site: http://www.cce.cornell.edu/publications/catalog.html

This publication is issued to further Cooperative Extension work mandated by acts of Congress of May 8 and June 30, 1914. It was produced with the cooperation of the U.S. Department of Agriculture; Cornell Cooperative Extension; and College of Agriculture and Life Sciences, College of Human Ecology, and College of Veterinary Medicine at Cornell University. Cornell Cooperative Extension provides equal program and employment opportunities. D. Merrill Ewert, Director.

Alternative formats of this publication are available on request to persons with disabilities who cannot use the printed format. For information call or write the Office of the Director, Cornell Cooperative Extension, 365 Roberts Hall, Ithaca, NY 14853 (607-255-2237).

Produced by Media and Technology Services at Cornell University

Printed on recycled paper

141IB23 20M ML MTS90034